How to Survive in Arkansas Prisons

Jimmie Ray Northern

Cadmus Publishing
www.cadmuspublishing.com

Copyright © 2023 Jimmie Ray Northern

Published by Cadmus Publishing
www.cadmuspublishing.com
Port Angeles, WA

ISBN: 978-1-63751-413-9
Library of Congress Control Number: 2023910603

All rights reserved. Copyright under Berne Copyright Convention, Universal Copyright Convention, and Pan-American Copyright Convention. No part of this book may be reproduced, stored in a retrieval system, or transmitted in any form, or by any means, electronic, mechanical, photocopying, recording or otherwise, without prior permission of the author.

Inside this book you will learn how to survive the rough terrain of the Arkansas prison system. You can use this knowledge to your advantage so you can have a blueprint that will help you overcome any obstacle in prison.

With this book you will discover the secret unwritten rules of the penitentiary! How to get through Hoe Squad! How to qualify for Act 309 and the work release programs, and much, much more! If you are facing prison time, this must-have manual will give you all the game!

Author's Note

My name is Jimmie Ray Northern #113936. I am a convict serving a 41-year prison sentence for second degree murder. I have done over 22 years in Arkansas' most dangerous penitentiaries. Here are a few of the units I have served time in.

Cummins Unit, Delta Regional unit, Calico Rock Unit, Act 309 Program at Lee County, Tucker Max Unit, Mississippi County Work Release Unit, Varner Super Max Unit, J.C.J. Unit, Pine Bluff Unit, Wrightsville Unit, and Brickeys Unit.

I wrote this manual to help you in your transition from becoming a shorthair to that of a convict. Inside these walls what you don't know can hurt you. The rules are totally different from those in the free world.

It's said that experience is a good teacher, but in prison you don't have a long time to learn, so it's best to seek the knowledge of someone who has already traveled this road and has done the hard work for you. Once you have mastered this place, then you have graduated the School of Hard Knocks. The system is not designed to initiate positive change in inmates. That's up to the individual. To continue down the same path that led you to prison is insanity. Different results require different thinking and reasoning.

J.R. Northern

Table of Contents

Chapter 1: Diagnostics Unit Intake 1
Chapter 2: Assigned Unit 4
Chapter 3: Your Appearance 6
Chapter 4: Look, Listen, and Learn 7
Chapter 5: Hoe Squad 9
Chapter 6: Your Living Area 11
Chapter 7: Classification 13
Chapter 8: Different Jobs 15
Chapter 9: Store Call 17
Chapter 10: Chow Hall 19
Chapter 11: Setting Goals 21
Chapter 12: Violence 22
Chapter 13: Different Prison Gangs 23
Chapter 14: If You Are Affiliated 24
Chapter 15: The Hole 25
Chapter 16: Ad-Seg 28
Chapter 17: I.D. Badge 30
Chapter 18: Disciplinaries 31
Chapter 19: Visitation 33
Chapter 20: Yard Call 35
Chapter 21: Church Call 36
Chapter 22: Gym Call 37
Chapter 23: Shakedowns and Strip Searches 38
Chapter 24: The Food 40
Chapter 25: Courses to Take 41
Chapter 26: Protective Custody 43
Chapter 27: Correctional Officers 45
Chapter 28: How a Barrack Looks Inside 46

Chapter 29: Drugs. 48
Chapter 30: Enemy Alert 50

Chapter 1

Diagnostics Unit Intake

Once you are shipped off from the county jail you will be headed to a Diagnostics Unit Intake. Upon your arrival you will be placed in a long line of inmates and one by one you will have your property inventoried.

You will be limited to only five pictures, a bible, and you get to keep the stack of mail you had from your county jail. They will then call you to a big, open, walk-in shower and have you strip down naked to be searched. The normal routine shakedown procedure. You will be asked to open your mouth wide, lift your tongue while the ADC officer looks around your mouth with a small flashlight.

You then will be asked to run your fingers through your hair to ensure no contraband is hidden inside. You will be asked to wiggle your fingers, then you will have to raise each foot and wiggle your toes and show them the soles of your feet. They will ask you then to lift your nut sack and then bend over and spread your butt cheeks, then cough.

Once that's done, you will have your groin area, armpits, and hair sprayed with anti-lice spray and then given a bar of state soap and asked to step into the shower where you are given 10 minutes to shower. You will then be given a towel to dry off with and given a new pair of boxers.

You will then be put in a long line of more inmates waiting to get your first penitentiary haircut, or should I say shaving, because they will shave all your hair off your head and face. You will then be headed to yet another long line of inmates to have your photo taken for your inmate I.D. badge. After that's done you will be issued a two-piece state icy white set of clothes with your last name stenciled on the front and a pair of socks and canvas shoes.

While at the Diagnostics Unit you will be tested for STDs, high cholesterol, and you will have your blood taken for DNA testing. You will get your eyes examined, your hearing will be tested, you will be given an all-over body physical to ensure you have no ailments or limited movement that will restrict you from working. If you pass the physical test, you will be required to work Hoe Squad. If you don't pass it, then you get to be building utility and only work inside.

The last thing you will do is be assigned a mental health counselor. You will be asked questions about if you ever abused drugs or alcohol. If you ever contemplated suicide or ever suffered from depression. In the event that you have a life-threatening trauma in the ADC would you want ADC to do all they could to save you or would you want them to pull the plug?

You will be asked your next of kin in case of an emergency. All these things will have taken about two weeks before you will be shipped to your first unit.

CHAPTER 2

ASSIGNED UNIT

Once you touch down at your assigned unit, you and the rest of the group that came with you will be taken to classification to be given cut slips that will tell you your job title and what barracks and bed number you will get. The majority of the group will all be placed on Hoe Squad.

In the beginning of your sentence, it's mandatory that you complete 60 days of Hoe Squad. Before going to your barracks, you will all be marched down the hallway to the laundry where they will issue you a mat, one pillow, one pillowcase, two bed sheets, one blanket, two sets of clothes, and one pair of boots.

If it's winter time, you will also be given two sets of thermal tops and bottoms, one state jacket, and one state hat. When placed in your barracks get on your assigned rack. Don't stop to kick it with your homies. If you happen to notice someone you recognize, just greet them and acknowledge them, then tell them that you will get with them later, but you have to get your house in order first.

By you going straight to your rack and getting your house in order it gives off a sense of confidence in yourself. Now on the other hand, if you stop and kick it with your homies and just sit your mat on the floor and mingle with your homies, it gives off the notion that you are looking for help and that you can't stand on your own. In the penitentiary you will be tested if they sense any kind of weakness in you. Don't try and be something you're not, just be yourself.

Chapter 3

Your Appearance

Don't wear your clothes skintight. Get a size that's not too loose but not too tight. No skinny jeans in here. You do not want anyone checking you out, so don't put yourself in that kind of situation. Always practice good hygiene. If you have a moustache, keep it trimmed but don't ever shave it off and go bald-faced because most homosexuals in the penitentiary keep their face completely clean shaven. You don't want to send out the wrong signals. Always try not to do too much smiling. Keep a sincere appearance, that way you don't look too friendly.

Chapter 4

Look, Listen, and Learn

No horse playing or joking around. A lot of people can dish it out, but they can't take too much criticism. Beware of anyone who gets too touchy-feely, always slap-boxing with you or trying to wrestle you. Believe me, that person has some kind of angle aimed at you. Don't fall for it. Nip that shit in the bud real quick.

Don't do too much talking. Less is better. By keeping your mouth shut and listening you will learn way more than running off at the mouth. Sit back and check out the scenery. Don't talk about your charge and don't ask nobody else what they are in prison for. It's considered rude and makes people uncomfortable.

Don't stare at anyone for too long. That will get you in a fight. Always lock your locker box. Remember, this is prison, and the lock will only keep the innocent people out of your box because a thief will get in it anyways. Don't accept gifts from anyone in prison. It might be a setup of some kind.

The penitentiary's full of all kinds of trick bag games aimed at shorthairs and you could get yourself caught up. Don't ask to borrow nobody's radio, MP4 player, or anything valuable because they could let you borrow it and then have their homeboy steal it from you and set you up to be indebted to them. If you ain't got the money to replace the property, then they are gonna want to be paid some kind of way. Feel me? Or they could give you some outrageous price that's three times the amount of their property. You got guys in the penitentiary that don't get money in on their books, so this is their hustle. Don't be a victim.

Chapter 5

Hoe Squad

Hoe Squad is hard work, so get a good night's sleep. Start you a workout program. Do a lot of back arms because it will help strengthen your arms to keep the stamina of Hoe Squad. Buy some work gloves to help protect your hands. Always wear two pair of socks so that it will cushion your feet from all the walking. Never wear tennis shoes to Hoe Squad unless you have a tennis shoe script from the infirmary. Try not to get in the middle of the Hoe Squad line.

You have the lead row and the tail row. The lead row is the beginning or start of the line and the tail row is the end of the line. Try to get close to either one but stay out of the middle of the Hoe Squad line. The middle does the most work. Get beside somebody that got some work in them or you will be getting their grass and yours. You can receive a major disciplinary for not getting your grass. Get that grass or lose your class!

When Hoe Squad is over, try to beat as much mud as you can off your boots before tracking all that mud back into the building or under your rack. Always hydrate the day before because drinking too much water while working the Hoe Squad will cramp you up and have you water-logged. Once you get in shape Hoe Squad will feel like yard call instead of work. Never approach the Hoe Squad rider on the horse, you will be shot. The proper way is to ask for permission to approach. Before you approach, lay your hoe down on the ground, then stay within 10 feet away from the officer on the horse, then state your request.

Chapter 6

Your Living Area

Keep your living area clean at all times. Keep your bed made if you are not laying in it. Make sure that you keep under your bed clean as well. Always keep an extra set of bed sheets and pillowcases so that while you are getting one set washed you will always have one set clean. You are a reflection of your living area, so remove the clutter and wash your sheets and pillowcases every week.

Don't hang anything on the walls. Never make it a habit of allowing anyone to get things out of your locker box. If you happen to give someone a soup or a shot of coffee, then you get it out of your box and give it to them. By avoiding this habit, you are making it harder for someone to steal from you. Don't leave any of your valuables like your new shoes, radio, MP4 player, watch, or magazines out laying around. If you are not using them lock them inside your locker box. Keep your box locked at all times. A thief is a patient opportunist because he will wait you out until you take that split second to go to the restroom, shower, or to chow call to get you.

It's better to be safe than sorry. By keeping your living area clean it will be harder for someone to plant contraband on you like a cell phone or shank. A shank is a penitentiary-made knife and if caught in your possession could cause you to lose your class.

Chapter 7

Classification

After completing your 60-day Hoe Squad you will be put up for a job change, so speak up for yourself. Let the warden know your qualifications like welding, maintenance, barber, cook, or whatever kind of work you did in the free world.

Do not go to Classification with your hair braided or in dreads unless you can produce a script showing Rastafarian affiliation. Always remember to state your name and your ADC number before you say anything, and remember to say, "yes, sir," and "yes, ma'am," or "no, sir," and "no, ma'am," when talking to Classification. Don't be sagging! Pull your pants up and look presentable. You want to present a good first impression because it could be the determining factor between a barracks porter job and a class 1-B job. A class 1-B job has benefits. Once you hold it for the first year-and-a-half you could be eligible for a weekend furlough.

Chapter 8

Different Jobs

There are many different jobs and job titles in the penitentiary. All jobs are not created equal. The top-of-the-line jobs are the class 1-B status jobs because they require minimum supervision, but you must earn these jobs by having a good institutional record and a good work history as well.

Here are the jobs of the ADC:
Laundry
Hall Porter
Kitchen
Barber
Barracks Porter
Sanitation
Hoe Squad
Major's Porter

Chaplain's Porter
Law Library Clerk
1-B Horse Barn
1-B Outside Maintenance
Inside Maintenance
1-B Front Office Porter
1-B Regional Maintenance
1-B Warden's Domestic
1-B Tractor Driver
Commissary

CHAPTER 9

STORE CALL

Commissary is necessary! When you first get placed in a barracks and you have plenty of money on your books, don't spend the whole $100 spending limit at store call. Spend just enough to eat for you, like about 10 soups, one bag of coffee, one box of cakes, and don't forget to buy some work gloves.

By you being frugal you are not setting yourself up to get robbed. Give yourself time to see what kind of barracks you are in first. Who knows, you might be in a barracks full of thieves. If you come strutting through the door every commissary day with the entire $100 store call limit, somebody's gonna try you.

Commissary is like free-world money and just like in the free world you got guys that will rob you in a heartbeat. Don't get caught up in the two-for-one game! If you happen to borrow 10 soups, one bag of coffee, and one box of cakes off the guy that's running a store in your barracks, be prepared to pay double back. So, be cautious of what you borrow or get from someone. Don't be a victim.

CHAPTER 10

CHOW HALL

When in the chow hall never leave your tray or drink unattended. If sitting at the picnic-style tables always sit straddling the seat with one leg under the table and one leg out just in case something jumps off. You do not want to get caught trapped at the table. Eat your food and get out of the chow hall. Don't do too much socializing.

Don't break line. Pay attention to your surroundings. Don't just sit anywhere. Make sure it's okay. To be safe, sit by someone you know or someone you are cool with that's in your barracks. Don't get caught trying to get back in the chow line for an extra tray. That's a disciplinary if caught.

Don't wear your shower shoes to the chow hall. You will be turned around and told to get in compliance. Never go to the chow hall without your state shirt on or with shorts on. You will be turned around. Remember to leave your wave cap in the barracks. If worn in or to the chow hall it will be confiscated and a disciplinary will be written.

Chapter 11

Setting Goals

If you are a short timer with 10 years or less, after being at your assigned unit for six months disciplinary free you can apply for Act 309 depending that you weren't charged with first degree murder, kidnapping, or rape.

The Act 309 program allows inmates that have a good institutional jacket and good work ethic to work in county jails. It's considered a class 1-A job, meaning that it's in the free world. Once you get within 30 months of your T.E. date you can apply for work release. Once you are chosen for work release you will be given a free world job. You will have an opportunity to leave prison with a nice-sized bankroll to make your transition back into society that much easier.

All of these opportunities can be yours if you make it a habit of setting goals and staying committed to your plan.

Chapter 12

Violence

Always remember you are in a prison setting and at any given time the whole room could erupt into some form of violence. In prison, at some point in time you will have to fight. Be respectful and you will be respected.

Stand up for yourself. In prison if you are soft, then you are gonna be preyed upon. You got to have a sense of hardness about yourself. Don't be the weakest link. As long as people know you will fight, they will be less likely to try you. They would rather take their chances with someone that's too scared to fight.

Chapter 13

Different Prison Gangs

Crips
Bloods
G.D.s
B.D.s
Vice Lords
M.S.-13s
Mexican Mafias
A.B.s
A.C.s
N.A.E.s
W.A.R.s

Chapter 14

If You Are Affiliated

At some point in time while in prison you are gonna be called upon to put in work for your set. You have active members and nonactive. If you are an active member of a gang, you are gonna have to get on count.

Once you are accounted for you will be required to know all the members of your affiliation, your history or knowledge, and you will be held accountable by your set or affiliation. In the event that you violate any of the rules set by your affiliation you will have to take a violation.

Violations are disciplinary measures kept to maintain discipline and order for prison gang members.

Chapter 15

The Hole

    The hole is where you are sent to sit out your sentence for any disciplinary you are found guilty of. There are single-man cells and there are two-man cells. Rule number one when sharing a two-man cell is don't ever cell with a known homosexual or anyone that is openly gay or anyone in question. It's a bad look.

    You don't want anyone getting the wrong idea because most homosexuals are known to make up lies and there goes your reputation. Don't ever cell with anyone that doesn't look right in the head. You are gonna be trusting this person with your life because at some time you will have to go to sleep. So, if a person don't look right, then don't let them come in your cell and by no means go in a cell with them.

In a two-man cell you are gonna have to learn how to cell because it's very rude to openly fart in a two-man cell. It's considered disrespectful. If you feel like you got to let one rip, get up and sit on the toilet, and just when you are about to let it rip, start flushing the toilet to shoot that gas down the toilet and out your room.

Flushing the toilet drowns out the noise as well. Your cell mate will be very appreciative and know that you are not a shorthair because you know how to cell.

If you have to do number two and your cell mate's asleep, tap his bunk and wake him up before sitting on the toilet. No one wants to be awakened by a flushing toilet and your cell mate taking a dump. When you wake him up you are being respectful because then he can turn his back to you if he stays on his bunk or he can go to the front of the cell and turn his back to you to give you your privacy.

Remember to drop one, sink one. That means to flush the toilet repeatedly. It removes nearly all the gas out of the air. Nobody wants to smell it, so keep it flushing. While you are in a two-man cell you got to maintain good hygiene practices. Your shower days will either be Monday, Wednesday, and Friday or Tuesday, Thursday, and Saturday. In between those days take a wash up and change out those boxers. You should have an extra pair to wear while one pair is being washed.

On the in-between days when you and your cell mate take turns taking your wash ups the procedure is just like when it's time to do number two. Either you lay in your bed and turn your back to your cell mate while he takes his wash up or you go to the front of the cell and turn your back to your cell mate until he's finished his wash up. You and your cell mate will have to be on the same page, so pay attention when he's trying to sleep. Don't be shouting and talking over the tier and he will give you the same respect. In the summer months temperatures will get way up in the 90s and hotter. In a two-man cell the smallest disagreement could start a fight, so don't do too much talking.

Chapter 16

Ad-Seg

When placed on administrative segregation you will be housed in the max part of the prison. The max is for violent offenders who have assaulted correctional officers or other inmates. If you catch too many disciplinaries back-to-back you will be assigned to ad-seg.

While in ad-seg you will be placed on single-man status, meaning you will have a cell all to yourself. You will be given a jumpsuit. You will be allowed one hour out of your cell each day for yard call recreation. The other 23 hours of the day you will be locked down in your cell.

The only time you will leave your cell is for sick call, dentist, classification, or video visits. All your meals will be brought to you by a correctional officer from a chow cart. Ad-seg has its pros and cons. The positive thing is you'll have your own cell to yourself and more privacy than being in general population. The negative thing about ad-seg is all the cell warrioring that goes on behind the doors. It's very loud and noisy. Plus, you can't spend that much on commissary weekly while on ad-seg. In general population you can spend $100 weekly at commissary.

Chapter 17

I.D. Badge

Your I.D. badge serves many different purposes in the penitentiary. You will need it to go to commissary, to receive your mail, to walk down the hallway. It is to be worn on a chain around your neck at all times. Without one you will not be allowed to go to commissary.

In the event you lose your I.D. you can go to the captain's office and have a computer printout that's to be used temporarily. At any given time you could be pulled over while in the hallways and if you don't have your I.D. badge you will be given a disciplinary for not being in compliance.

CHAPTER 18

DISCIPLINARIES

A disciplinary has the famous name of Mellow Yellow. You don't want to get too many of these because it ruins your chances of going to work release, 309, or getting a decent job. The one disciplinary you want to definitely avoid getting is a 10-3, or as it's called a Dime Charge.

A 10-3 or Dime Charge is when an inmate is written up for masturbation while looking at a female correctional officer. Try to avoid this disciplinary because if you get too many within a year's time then they will make you register as a sex offender.

Plus, whenever your family Googles your institutional jacket to see your disciplinary history it will say Sexual Act instead of a 10-3 charge. When people in the free world see sexual act they are gonna think you are in prison having homosexual relations. It's good to know all the rules and regulations to limit your chance of getting a disciplinary.

Chapter 19

Visitation

On visitation you are allowed a kiss and a hug upon meeting your visitors and a kiss and a hug when they are leaving. The rules governing inmate visits are strictly enforced. In order to get a visit from anyone they must be accepted on your approved visitation list. Visits will not be scheduled on a holiday unless the holiday occurs on the inmate's regular scheduled visitation day.

Visits for inmates assigned to administrative segregation may be arranged by contacting the visitation office. These visits will be conducted in a more secure setting. Inmates assigned to punitive status may be permitted to receive visits of two hours one time per month. These visits must be requested at least 24 hours in advance and must be approved by the warden.

All persons, property, and vehicles will be subject to search. All applicants will be subject to a criminal background check. No more than four people can visit during a visitation period. No provocative or inappropriate clothing will be permitted. No halter tops, tank tops, hats, shorts, mini-skirts, see-through clothing, or camouflage attire may be worn.

No sleeveless tops are allowed. Your shoulders must be covered at all times. Children 10 years of age and under will be allowed to wear shorts of appropriate length. Visitors can't give you money, gifts, or food. If caught furnishing any prohibited articles like tobacco, smoking paraphernalia, electronic communication devices, alcohol, or drugs you will be charged with a felony.

Visitors can only carry in a small coin purse, billfold, identification, baby bottle, baby diapers, wipes, car keys, and jewelry.

Chapter 20

Yard Call

If you want to minimize your chances of being involved in an altercation, stay clear of physical activities like prison basketball games. On the court the prison ball is played very, very aggressively and the majority of the players that compete are hotheads.

Always ask who's up next on the weight pile before picking up the dumbbells or any other weights. There's probably a line, so don't cause no unnecessary trouble for yourself.

Watch your surroundings because most times the yard will be packed and at any time something could go down, so be attentive. If you see a lot of inmates huddled up in an area, stay clear of them because it's probably a gang meeting.

Chapter 21

Church Call

If you decide to go to any church services always go in large groups. There will always be a nice number of people in your barracks that will get on the church call list.

Church is used as a way for gang members to all meet up and discuss prison politics. Watch where you decide to sit at in church because a lot of the different gangs will want to sit together. Don't get caught talking too loud in service. You could get a disciplinary.

When church call is over, they will let groups of 15 to 20 people out at a time. Make sure that you pay attention what group of 15 to 20 guys you are in because you could place yourself in harm's way by being with the wrong guys. Also stay attentive because the majority of the sneak attacks take place at church events. Try to sit up close to the first couple of benches.

Chapter 22

Gym Call

The gym will be normally packed with inmates playing basketball, lifting weights, and posted up all around the gym floor. The different gangs will use gym call as a way to meet up to discuss prison politics and have meetings and functions.

If you see a lot of guys huddled up in a large group talking, don't go near them. It's probably a gang meeting. Keep your eyes open and pay attention to the vibes because at any time all hell can break loose. Don't get jammed up on a contraband charge because you will be subject to a shakedown before leaving the gym, on your way through the hallways back to your barracks, and once you make it back to your barracks, so don't get caught riding dirty.

Chapter 23

Shakedowns and Strip Searches

 At any given time, the Dog Boys, Hoe Squad Riders, or the Emergency Response teams can and will run up in your barracks to do random, surprise shakedowns and strip searches. If you are caught in possession of any weapons, drugs, gang literature, or any contraband you will be given a disciplinary and taken to the hole for lock up.

 When they enter your barracks, you will all be asked to strip down to only your boxers and shower shoes and told to go to the dayroom. Once there they will call you one at a time to go to the restroom area where you will be stripped naked and told to squat and cough.

 Once you have gotten back dressed you then will be escorted to your assigned rack and have your entire property gone through looking for contraband. So, don't store anything for anyone because if you get caught with a weapon or drugs that you are hiding for someone, then you will get a disciplinary and those kind of disciplinaries will block you from going to work release or 309.

Chapter 24

The Food

    The food is nothing to write home about. There are some days you'll get a decent meal and then there are days when there's nothing on your tray that's tempting. So, make sure that you get a nice-sized bankroll on your books before coming to prison so you don't have to suffer the tasteless prison food.
    You may as well buy a lot of condiments like mayo, ketchup, mustard, jalapeno peppers, Louisiana hot sauce strips, Kraft ranch dressing, BBQ sauce, chopped onion, and pickles to give the food some taste. You can always buy some regular corn chips to go along with each meal. It's good to have a little commissary for any bad food days.

CHAPTER 25

COURSES TO TAKE

There are courses you can take that will look good in your institutional jacket and may give you favor when it's time for you to go in front of the Parole Board. If you have a drug charge, it will be good for you to sign up for a S.A.T.P. course.

S.A.T.P. course is a drug class and it's designed to help you cope and stay drug free. There's the anger management course. It will be good to take because it looks good in your jacket. You have the reentry program that's designed to help you make your transition back into society a success. They help you get your driver's license back reinstated and they prepare you for the free world.

Some reentry courses provide inmates with jobs that pay just like a work release program. You have a parenting class that teaches how to be an effective part in your children's lives.

You can't go wrong by getting in all of these courses. If you don't take any of these courses, the Parole Board will look at you and think that you just wasted your time in prison and that you didn't rehabilitate yourself and decide to give you a year denial.

Chapter 26

Protective Custody

If you just ain't got no heart, no fight, and you don't want no problems, and you could care less of what anyone ever thought or said about you, then P.C. or protective custody might not be too bad for you. After all, everybody can't handle the pressure of the prison system.

Although you must be forewarned that once you get a P.C. jacket on you, you will never be treated with real respect as a man while you are in the prison system. Being in P.C. says to everyone that you are not a real, true soldier. So, think about going that route.

A lot of guys that are afraid of the prison system who have small time will catch P.C. to cruise through their short sentence, but if they ever come back through the system everyone will always remember that they caught P.C., so do what's best for you.

Chapter 27

Correctional Officers

Just like anywhere else, you got some good C.O.s and some bad C.O.s. It's up to you how you start the relationship off. It don't take no rocket scientist to know that you don't piss off the people that have to feed you.

A real convict will treat any C.O. like he wants to be treated because everybody needs somebody, sometime. You never know what can and will happen, so try to stay on a positive note with the C.O.s if you can.

By you keeping a cordial relationship, you might get spared when you do get caught in the wrong, but if you are on their bad side, the smallest little infraction will result in disciplinary action.

Chapter 28

How a Barrack Looks Inside

The average barrack will hold about 56 inmates. You have a bottom tier and a top tier. There are 28 racks upstairs and 28 racks downstairs. You have the dayroom that has two televisions. One is the sports TV, the other one is the movie TV. The restroom area is to the side of the dayroom area.

There are four toilets, four sinks with mirrors, and a walk-in single-man shower. In the dayroom you will have two long benches for the sports TV and four long benches for the movie TV. In between the sports TV benches and the movie TV's benches are four tables that sit four people to each table. There are two phones on each side of the dayroom and two video screens for ordering commissary and having video visits at the front of the barracks on each side of the TV.

A water fountain is in the dayroom right next to the restroom area. There's a steel cage that's called a bullpen that has a gate that has to be opened electronically from master control to allow anyone leaving the barracks to leave out. Once you are inside the bullpen then the officer that's over that barrack will then open the barrack's front door to let you out.

In the front of the barracks is the barrack's control booth. An officer can oversee two barracks at a time. At one end of the control booth is one barrack and at the other end of the control booth is the other barrack. If anything serious jumps off inside your barracks, it's like a death trap because you can't get out. Sometimes master control takes their sweet little time to open the bullpen. So, be careful and try to avoid trouble if you can.

Chapter 29

Drugs

Stay drug-free in prison if you can because if you think being strung out on drugs is bad in the free world, then it's 10 times worse for you in the penitentiary. The most common drugs in the penitentiary are marijuana, meth, ice, K-2, sherm, and cocaine. Cigarettes are just as bad because they are addictive and bad for you as well.

When you get caught in possession of any of the above-named contraband it will lead to a disciplinary and even the possibility of catching a free world charge. The prices are sky high for cigarettes and drugs in prison. If you continue to indulge you can find yourself getting in over your head in debt.

That could lead to you putting yourself in harm's way because of your debt, so pass on all drugs and cigarettes. At any given time you could be given a random surprise drug test. If you test positive for any of the above drugs, then you can lose your class and that will only prolong your time in prison. If you get too many dirty urinalysis's then you will probably be looking at a year denial. The Parole Board will then stipulate that you take S.A.T.P. before you can be released. So, say no to drugs!

Chapter 30

Enemy Alert

If you are ever involved in any altercations while in prison, you and whoever you fought will be placed on each other's enemy alert. Enemy alert is designed to give an inmate the heads up alerting him of the dangers of being sneak attacked or retaliated on by some former enemy. So, if you are afraid for your safety because your victim's family members are housed at the same unit and you don't want no problems, you will have to alert the administration and have that person put on your enemy alert. Be cautious not to loan out a lot of your commissary on consignment because a lot of inmates will run up a huge tab and then put you on their enemy alert to avoid having to pay you back. Don't be a victim!

JIMMIE RAY NORTHERN

THE NUMBER ONE RULE IN PRISON IS...

(CONTINUED IN PART 2)

www.ingramcontent.com/pod-product-compliance
Lightning Source LLC
Chambersburg PA
CBHW071916070526
44583CB00016B/2011